**green press**
INITIATIVE

TWO HUNDRED NIGHTS AND ONE DAY

To Sharon

Margaret Rozga

with best writing wishes

Peggy Rozga

200 Nights

and one day

Foreword by Dick Gregory

Benu Press

09 10 11 12 7 6 5 4 3 2   FIRST EDITION

Cover design by Brian Mallman.
Cover photograph, Father James Groppi leading a fair housing march
in 1967, from the *Milwaukee Journal Sentinel,* Journal Sentinel Inc.,
reproduced with permission. *Wisconsin Historical Society* WHi-25167.

Book design by Claudia Carlson (www.claudiagraphics.com).
The text is set in Fairfield; the display script is Carlotta.

Author photograph by Barbara Reinhart.

Library of Congress Control Number: 2009920615

ISBN-13: 978-0-9815163-1-8
ISBN-10: 0-9815163-1-9

P.O. Box 5330
Hopkins, Minnesota 55343-9998
www.benupress.com

For Anna, Christine, and Matthew

Foreword

Two Hundred Nights and One Day is brilliantly delivered by author Margaret (Peggy) Rozga. This book of poetry presents a brilliant analysis which takes us through the brave history of the strength, commitment and passion of the people of Milwaukee, Wisconsin as they marched, struggled and were jailed to win the victory of justice and freedom for all. Peggy Rozga joined protestors, participated in freedom marches, and was jailed for fighting and marching for the rights of poor Black children of the city of Milwaukee under the leadership of one of the great advocates of non-violence, direct action and civil disobedience of our times: Father James Edmund Groppi.

Father Groppi had an empathy for the black poor folks and he wasn't going to rest until victory was won. A man of Italian descent who, as a White man, could have done whatever he chose in this privileged land called America, chose to truly be a man of God and fight the human fight for justice. He dedicated his life to the fight for equality for all.

Two Hundred Nights and One Day is as good as it gets. It is the record of the Civil Rights Movement, of the ingredients of how victories were won in Milwaukee, Wisconsin. This book is our history. It is a book of passion and love human beings fought for, whether they were Black or White. Father Groppi was an Italian brother born and raised in the city of Milwaukee in a middle-class family, but he could not accept the housing crisis, the segregation of the schools crisis, and the wrongs of our government.

I am honored to have been invited to march side by side with the people of Milwaukee in the name of justice. The

Bible says in Psalm 23, *"Yea, though I walk through the valley of the shadow of death, I will fear no evil: for thou art with me; thy rod and thy staff they comfort me."* This I so believe because God was with me when I joined the community freedom fighters of Milwaukee under the leadership of Father James Groppi as we marched hand in hand, together protesting the injustices. It has been my commitment not only as an activist to fight the wrongs of our government for the human rights of all people, but it is my commitment as a father, a husband and as a man of God to join forces with those who also contribute their intelligence, their hearts and passion to do the same. This book will make you feel the hunger, strength, sweat and victory of the marchers' fight and commitment for equality.

This is America. That day was America. And I am blessed to have been there with these freedom fighters as victory was fought for and won.

— Dick Gregory

I rebel; therefore we exist.

—Albert Camus
The Rebel

Chronology

OF THE OPEN HOUSING MOVEMENT IN MILWAUKEE

1956: Vel Phillips, first African American and first woman, elected to the Milwaukee Common Council

1960: Vel Phillips reelected

March, 1962: Vel Phillips introduces fair housing bill which is defeated with only her vote in favor.

1963–1967: Vel Phillips introduces fair housing bill three more times. Each time it is defeated with only her vote in favor.

1965: Father James Groppi appointed advisor to the Milwaukee Youth Council of the NAACP

1966: Milwaukee begins the Kilbourntown 3 redevelopment project, tearing down properties on the near north side, increasing the housing crunch for African American families.

Fall 1966: St. Boniface elementary school students attend trial of Milwaukee property owner Joseph Brown for building code violations on his inner city properties.

November 1966: Vietnam veteran, his wife, and infant daughter try to rent a flat near 29th and Burleigh. The owner refuses to rent to them. When they ask her if it's because they are African American, she says, "I can't rent to you. What would my neighbors think?"

The family denied housing bring their complaint to Fr. Groppi and the NAACP Youth Council. After trying unsuccessfully to negotiate with the owner, the Youth Council members go to the house and sing Christmas carols to the owner.

Spring 1967: The Youth Council pickets at the homes of alderman who have African American constituencies but who are voting against the fair housing bill. These aldermen include Martin Schreiber, Sr., president of the Common Council and Eugene Woehrer. The Youth Council also pickets at the law office of Alderman James Maslowski. These aldermen once again vote against the fair housing ordinance on June 14, 1967.

August 24, 1967: Youth Council members Prentice McKinney and Dwight Benning announce that the Youth Council has decided to march across the 16th Street Viaduct from Milwaukee's north side to Kosciuszko Park on Milwaukee's south side.

Monday, August 28, 1967: Youth Council members and supporters march through hostile crowds to Kosciuszko Park.

Tuesday, August 29, 1967: Police estimate that 13,000 counter-demonstrators gather on the route of the march. 250 Youth council members and supporters march to the Park. Police stay between the marchers and the hostile crowds and finally use tear gas to disperse the unruly White counter-demonstrators. The march ends at 8:30 p.m. at the north end of the Viaduct. Youth Council members return to their headquarters, the Freedom House at 1316 North 15th Street in the Kilbourntown 3 redevelopment area. At 9:30 p.m., police say they heard there's a sniper in the Youth Council Freedom House. The police fire tear gas canisters into the house; a blaze erupts and the house is burned beyond repair.

Wednesday, August 30, 1967: Mayor Maier issues a proclamation banning all marches between 4:00 p.m. and 9:00 a.m. for the next 30 days. In an effort to comply with the proclamation, the Youth Council cancels the scheduled march for that evening, deciding to have a rally at the burned-out Freedom House, but no march. 300 people show up for the rally. The police declare the assembly unlawful and arrest 58 persons.

Thursday, August 31, 1967: Youth Council holds a rally at St. Boniface Church, 2609 North 11th Street, Milwaukee, Wisconsin. Open housing supporters fill the church to overflowing. The decision is made to march despite the mayor's proclamation. When the march reaches 9th Street and North Avenue, less than a mile from the Church, the police move in to arrest the marchers. At least 140 adults and an unspecified number of juveniles are arrested and taken to the Police Safety Building in downtown Milwaukee or the juvenile detention center in Wauwatosa. The adults are fingerprinted and photographed. Bond for each person charged with violating the Mayor's proclamation is set at $25.00.

Friday, September 1, 1967: Youth Council holds an outdoor rally on the St. Boniface playground. For four and a half hours, they await word from a legal team in Madison trying to get an injunction against the mayor's proclamation. When Atty. Bill Coffey telephones to report they have been unsuccessful, the Youth Council once again decides to march anyway. Syd Finley, NAACP Region 3 Field Director, and Father Groppi lead the march. Police begin arresting marchers as soon as they move onto 12th Street. Then the police tear gas those still on the playground, lobbing the tear gas canisters over the heads of the crowd so that, as they try to return to the church, they run into the tear gas. On the other hand, if they run away from the tear gas, they run onto 12th Street and are arrested by the police.

Monday, September 4, 1967: Father Groppi and the Youth Council receive telegrams of support from national civil rights leaders including Rev. Martin Luther King.

Sunday, September 10, 1967: After the National NAACP office and various church groups put out calls for volunteers to come to Milwaukee to support the Youth Council, 5,000 people march in Milwaukee in support of the fair housing ordinance.

Tuesday, September 26, 1967: Vel Phillips re-introduces the fair housing ordinance, and it is referred to the Judiciary Committee of the Milwaukee Common Council.

Monday, October 31, 1967: The Judiciary Committee refuses to recommend any fair housing legislation to the Common Council.

November 1967–March 1968: Youth Council continues to march for open housing for over 200 nights.

February 1968: Senator Walter Mondale of Minnesota in a speech to the Congress in support of an open housing amendment specifically mentions Father Groppi and the Milwaukee marches.

April 4, 1968: Rev. Martin Luther King shot and killed in Memphis, Tennessee.

April 11, 1968: Federal open housing law passed.

April 30, 1968: After defeating it six times, the Milwaukee Common Council finally passes an open housing ordinance that equals and surpasses the coverage in the federal law.

Photos

FROM THE WISCONSIN HISTORICAL SOCIETY

Groppi Protesting Eagle's Club, 1966

Father James Groppi and the NAACP Youth Council demonstrating outside the Eagles Club at night beneath a marquee advertising a Duke Ellington performance. *Wisconsin Historical Society* WHi-53595

Freedom House Burning, 1967

Freedom House in flames after Milwaukee Police fired tear gas into the building. Two armed officers stand in front of the burning building. Both officers have gas masks on their heads. *Wisconsin Historical Society* WHi-48147

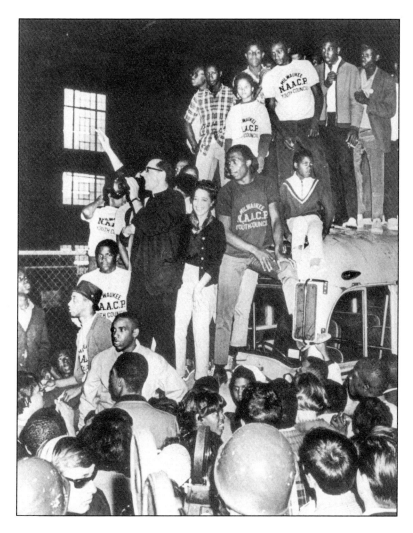

Father Groppi and Vel Phillips on Hood of Bus

Father James Groppi speaking through a megaphone from the hood of a bus. Groppi stands with Alderperson Vel Phillips. Several of the people in the assembled crowd wear Milwaukee NAACP Youth Council shirts. Visible in the foreground are persons in helmets filming the gathering. Photo: *Milwaukee Journal Sentinel,* Journal Sentinel Inc., reproduced with permission. *Wisconsin Historical Society* WHi-48419

Father James Groppi at NAACP March, 1968

Father James Groppi (1930–1985) and social activists at NAACP March, marching east up Wisconsin Avenue. Photo: Howard M. Berliant. *Wisconsin Historical Society* WHi-1912

Father James E. Groppi shortly after he was found guilty of obstructing an officer. Margaret Rozga is pictured to his right in the floral print dress. Photo: *Milwaukee Journal Sentinel,* Journal Sentinel Inc., reproduced with permission.

Father Groppi at School Boycott

Father James Groppi and students from Boniface School join the public school boycott. They're clapping their hands and appear to be chanting. *Wisconsin Historical Society* WHi-40697

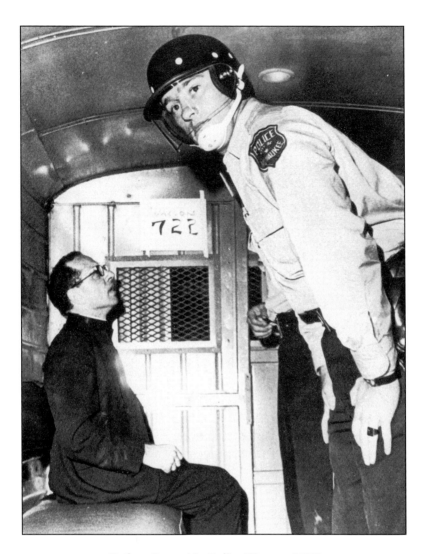

Father Groppi in Police Wagon, 1966

Father Groppi is seated in the back of a police wagon with policeman after being arrested in front of his parish for the second night in a row. *Wisconsin Historical Society* WHi-26541

Face-off Between Police and NAACP Members

The Milwaukee police approach a line of NAACP Youth Council members in an attempt to break up a demonstration. Photo: *Milwaukee Journal Sentinel,* Journal Sentinel Inc., reproduced with permission. *Wisconsin Historical Society* WHi-59547

Father Groppi Leads Demonstration

Father James Groppi, seen wearing sunglasses in the middle of a crowd, leads a demonstration against discrimination. *Wisconsin Historical Society* WHi-59546

Table of Contents

TWO HUNDRED NIGHTS AND ONE DAY

Prologue to Milwaukee

Before Milwaukee and south of Wisconsin

People on the march
boycotting buses,
no more pay up front
to go to the back, no more
sitting in the back. No more
looking down, looking away.
No more. No more.

People on the march
sitting in at lunch counters,
Greensboro, Nashville, denied service,
beaten, jailed, but their spirit
resists arrest. Advances.

People on the march
to the county courthouse,
Washington D.C.,
the Lincoln Monument, the Jefferson Memorial,
all the way from Selma to Montgomery,
Chicago into Cicero. Cicero?

History remembers the dream, forgets nightmares.
Those startled awake, stay awake,
remember, try again, march on, inspire
individual photos, moving pictures.

People on the march
moving north, Milwaukee,
moving into the heart of a young African American woman,

a lawyer, married to a lawyer, but they live with negatives:
block-busting; restrictive covenants.

People on the march
moving a young African American man,
a Marine, returned from Vietnam,
seeking a home for his family,
told by the owner, *I can't rent to you.*
What would my neighbors think?

People on the march
moving the heart and soul of a White
Roman Catholic priest at St. Boniface Church.
He listened to the Vietnam veteran.
He watched the young African American woman
win election to the City Council,
introduce a fair housing bill,
vote alone for that bill
time after time after time.

People on the march
moving into the deepest fiber of the teenagers
playing basketball on neighborhood playgrounds,
the young adults on the streets who could not find work.
Not the Milwaukee of *Happy Days*
though it is that same time, that same place.

People on the march
moving history into drama.

The setting:
Milwaukee, St. Boniface Catholic Church,
the 16th Street Viaduct,

the 15th Street Freedom House, Kosciusko Park,
Wisconsin Avenue, city hall, the city jail.

The cast of characters:
people, young and old, Black and White
powerful and challenging power,
cowardly and courageous,
stodgy and on the move.

The plot:
wind from the south, south east.
Dreams, nightmares, closed doors, closed still.
The rising action, the turning point,
the denouement.
Lights, camera, action.
Two hundred nights of marching.
People on the march.

Milwaukee.
An epilogue maybe in your steps,
maybe the other side of the long expanse
of bridge you think you can't cross.

Pam Learns Math

My grandmother put us in St. Boniface School.
Wanted us to learn, No better place to learn.

Father Groppi walked right into our seventh grade, said,
Come on, you all. We're going downtown.

Took us to the Courthouse, high-class slum lord
on trial. Multiple building code violations
on each of his one hundred properties. Fined.
One dollar for the whole lot of them.

We learned.
Learned each code violation
costs less than a penny. Learned
how easy it is to screw the poor.

Learned school doesn't want you to see the real thing.
The Sisters, oooh, Sister Kathleen was mad, ran after him,
after us, yelling, *You need permission slips.* Wagging her finger
in the air. *Parents need to be notified.* Warning *Next time....*

She didn't get to finish. We learned even
before St. Boniface, you get your chance to go,
don't hang around waiting for someone to say no.
Go.

Next time Father did permission slips.
Our parents signed; they didn't have a problem.
They were ready.

We went to the Common Council meeting.
Watched Vel Phillips introduce her open housing law.
All the aldermen

talking their rights, their property, their constituents,
their questions, their concerns, their votes against her bill.

Only Vel voted for open housing.
We went to see our government in action.
Our representatives vote against us. We learned.

The Lone Vote

Vel R. Phillips, first African American
and first woman, elected to the
Milwaukee Common Council, April 1956

A house. To buy a house. To start a family.
A chance to buy a house near good schools.

It should have been a matter of course.
We earned enough, practicing law together,
Dale, my husband, and I,
but there we were, living above a drugstore.

We'd call realtors, who said they'd call right back,
but our phone number started with 372-....
That was all they needed to hear.
We had to be Negro. They'd never call back.

Milwaukee, the 1950s, post war building boom,
Jackie Robinson playing in the majors,
the Boston Braves move to Milwaukee, then
Henry Aaron, a hard time seeking housing.

Frank, Mayor Frank Ziedler, built public housing.
I wanted fair housing. How to be heard?
How to open doors? Who, how, when?

I joined the League of Women Voters
worked on their campaign for state-wide
re-apportionment, thirty years overdue,
Blacks woefully underrepresented.

But the wording of the referendum was confusing.
Deliberately done that way.

If you were for reapportionment, you had to vote no.
If you were against reapportionment, you were to vote yes.
The League was concerned that people in favor
would vote yes, thinking yes meant yes.

I was introduced to poverty going door to door
explaining reapportionment. Two houses on a lot,
houses facing the back alleys. Some people told me
they don't vote, couldn't vote back in Arkansas.

I had to tell them they could vote here,
where to vote, what the vote
on reapportionment meant: being heard,
being counted. Power to open doors.

Run for alderman? Dale said no, he
didn't care to run, so I did. And I won.

I did my homework, learned how things worked,
how I could work. Used the aldermen's bathroom.
Refrained from correcting their English
when they talked the d's: dese, dem, dose, dat.

The worst of them thought highly of himself.
A gentleman farmer, owned a nursery. He said
Vel, I wouldn't mind your living next to me.

I looked at him squarely and asked
What makes you think I'd want you living next to me?

After I was re-elected I introduced
a fair housing ordinance. First time in 1962.
Three more times in the next four years. Each time
mine was the only vote in favor.

No national attention, no local attention. Nothing.
Until the marches. White priest, black youth.
COMMANDOs. That got attention.
National news. All over. Marches.

My mother didn't want me to march.
She didn't think it was ladylike. When I was arrested,
she didn't go to church that Sunday.
She was too embarrassed.

Dale didn't want me to march either.
But sometimes there are things you just have to do.
Sometimes you have to stand up for yourself.
Sometimes you stand alone but alone doesn't matter

if you're standing up for others.

RESPECT

Ronald and Norma Britton, December 1966

It was a well-built brick house, but Norma,
Norma seemed uneasy. She checked
and rechecked the ad, the address.
Okay. But I wonder why there's no for rent sign up here.

What worried her now? I survived Vietnam.
Our daughter is healthy, ten pounds already. We have
money for rent. We'll be able to save for a down payment.
Doesn't look like any Negroes on the block.

Hey, it's winter. Folks are inside.
We have laws now. Martin Luther King.
Norma, Norma, I fought for my country.
Things have changed.

Right. She smiles. I walk around the car,
give her a hand, help her with the baby.

A White woman answers the door.
We'd like to see the flat you advertised for rent.
Yes, the downstairs unit.

Rented? Already?
It was in this afternoon's paper.
You say what?
You couldn't cancel the ad that quick?

You're worried about what? About
what would your neighbors think?

Norma and I look at each other.
At our daughter.
At the door closing.

This is No Metaphor. This is Real

Here it is Christmas.
And here is a good Christian woman

at church every Sunday. At Christmas
she donates extra to decorate the church.

At midnight Mass she shivers,
hears about Jesus born in a stable.

Hard-hearted innkeepers had no room
for Joseph, for Mary who is with child.

Why doesn't that priest stay where he belongs,
in the pulpit to preach this gospel?

Milwaukee Talks

Did you hear? Father Groppi got a new car.
Oh, yeah? What kind?
A black demonstrator.

You Do the Math

About 20 of us picketed James Maslowski, realtor alderman
not in at either of his offices. About 40 of us picketed Alderman

Martin Schreiber, Senior, Common Council president, where
we were politely received but told by the Alderman

that he would not vote for a fair housing bill.
About 50 of us picketed at the home of Alderman

Robert Dwyer, whose daughter answered the door,
asked what we wanted, and said her father, the alderman,

was not home. Next up, Eugene Woehrer who appeared
then disappeared. So we marched around the block of this alderman

picking up supporters until we numbered well over one hundred,
Our support was growing on the very block of the alderman's

home. Yet even Peabody can't figure it. The number
voting for fair housing remained the same. One. Alderwoman.

Peggy Figures It Out

Restrict-
ive covenants
Even her neighborhood
divided by design. Don't ask
Don't tell.

Shirley's Mother

June 1967

The police took pictures of us
every picket line, every demonstration.
Then they started to follow us home,
park right in front, so we'd know
they were watching, watching us,
taking pictures of us coming and going.

What about the Constitution, I wanted to know.

One day a big late model sedan, unmarked,
two burly White men in rumpled suits in the front seat,
parked smack across the street from our house.
I went right out there and asked them,
Do you live in this neighborhood?

No, ma'am.

Well, what are you doing here?
Well?
I'm waiting. You need to answer me.
Parked and watching my house, my daughters.
What you watching us for?
What you watching my daughters for?
You some kind of perverts, stalking my daughters?
Are you the police?

Ma'am, you're obstructing traffic, standing in the street.

I don't see any cars on this street
but yours. Who am I obstructing?
You talk like the police. You the police?
Or you some kind of perverts?

Well, I'm calling the police.
I've got to protect my neighborhood.
I went right in and called the police.
Called the police on the police.
Sure did.

Shirley

I am the middle child.
I have two brothers and one sister older than myself.
I have three younger sisters.

I am in the middle of my family,

and I was born on Wednesday,
the middle of the week.

I am Akua Ekua,
a name that comes from Ghana.
I am a peacemaker.
I have the ability to make people famous.
I am a builder of nations.

Arrest the White Girls

Just as I put my foot on the clutch
to downshift my little Rambler
into the turn, I saw the sign,
no left turns.

Then flashing red and blue lights.

The cops made us park, get out,
took us downtown, put my sister Jeannie
and me each in a separate room.
Questioned us: *What were you doing*

there?

I was so scared.
In a separate room
with them,
without my sister.
Why were you in

that neighborhood?

Questions like that.

Before letting us call our parents,

they brought us together.

You girls should stay away from
there.

You don't know what you're doing,
hanging around with

those people.

In that moment something
overwhelming filled the room.
I could see the unsaid word
try to wrap its tentacles around us.

Where Lawrence Learns the Law

South 50ᵗʰ Street

Cops were always parked right
in front of the Freedom House.
Saying there were threats against us.
They had to protect us.

Yeah, they protecting us,
but we the only ones going to jail.
One night, they arrested a girl
for throwing her cigarette on the sidewalk.

We went outside to see what was going on,
they arrested us, too. Took us downtown.
Fingerprinted us. Photographed us.
Yeah, for dropping a cigarette.

So we had to return the favor, right?
Drove out to Chief Breier's house
I'll never forget that address.

We parked in that all-White neighborhood,
sat out there all night. Guarding the Chief of Police.
Hey, there'd been threats against him.
We didn't want anything to happen to him.

Next night we're out there again.
What thanks do we get?
We're arrested
for guarding the chief of police
without a private detective's license.

Inner City

They took me into an interrogation room, kept
calling me Robert, which usually only nuns did.

Asked me if Father Groppi was planning a riot.
I just shook my head. They were crazy.

Asked me what I thought of Father Groppi.
I said *I love him.*
I love the quicksand he walks on.

July 31, 1967

Want to know how the riot started?

There were these guys from Chicago.
There was this dance at St. Francis Church.
There was a big crowd. Lots of fun.
There was Tommy Lee with his good shoes.

There were these guys, these Chicago guys
there looking for a fight.
There he went and did it. One of them stepped on Tommy Lee's shoes.
There. His good shoes. New. Dress shoes. Fine black leather.
　　Oooo ooo.
There was no way Tommy Lee would let them get away with that.
There was the door. I had to get him out of
there. The dance was over anyway. Everyone,
they're out on the street. On 4th street, 4th and Brown.

There were these Chicago guys still bothering us. Down to Third Street,
there was trouble, trouble starting. Pretty soon everyone's mixing
　　it up. That
there was the one place I didn't want to be. I had to get out of
there. Get home. Good thing I lived right up on 6th Street. Walked in,
there's my grandmother: *'bout time, Pam.* We watched the news,
　　already it's
there on the TV: civil disturbance on Third Street. Before I'm asleep,

Mayor Maier's calling the National Guard in there.

Curley's Verdict

I got arrested on North Avenue.
Just happened to be out, didn't know
there was a riot on Third Street.
Martial law.

Went before Judge Christ Seraphim.
You know, the one who told Father Groppi
Milwaukee is not Mississippi
The one who said *you will not overcome.*

He started lecturing.
Robert, you have to work,
you have to obey the law.
Kept going on and on.

I hadn't done a thing,
but he didn't know, didn't care.
Didn't care to ask if I had a job
which I did.

It got to me, all his nagging,
squawking, crowing, rapping.
Strange bird, this judge.

I said to him,
I hear your daughter's pregnant by a Black man.
That just popped out of my mouth.
Words cutting swift and deep

somehow saved me though he got mad.
Jaw got all tight, face all red.
Started sputtering, fluttering, carrying on.

They took me out of his court room, you know,
took me right out there to the House of Correction.
Kept me three days for psychiatric evaluation.

Never more.

City Limits

You wouldn't know the city was under a curfew
not here, not on this southern edge of Milwaukee,
where I grew up. Where I still lived.

After supper, people did their usual.
Next door Mr. Stanisch cut his grass, as he did every other day,
alternating with setting out the sprinklers to water the lawn.

Mrs. Selinski sent Kathy up to the corner store for sweet rolls.
The Campions came into the Dutchland Dairy where I
    worked part-time.
It was hot. They bought half a gallon of fresh frozen custard.
    Vanilla.

The cop who lived across the street
never brought little Frankie in for a treat.
His lawn seemed to stay clipped without being mowed.
His wife had a bad heart. We didn't see much of her.

Maybe he worked overtime during the riot, again for the
    marches.
It was hard to say when he was home. Our paths didn't cross.
Except once. A year earlier, he had a point to make.

My friends from the Youth Council had stopped by.
Next evening Sgt. Bruskowiak crossed 44th Street
when I was alone in the front yard.

Your friends
are more than welcome in

my neighborhood
as long as they
behave themselves.

Point made, he turned, took firm, flat-footed steps
back across the street to his house,
the impregnable prose of his lannon stone colonial.

His neighborhood.

The Bridge

What's the longest bridge in the world?
The 16th Street Viaduct. It connects Africa and Poland.

—old Milwaukee joke

Reporting the Numbers

Bernice Buresh, *The Milwaukee Sentinel*
Tuesday, August 29, 1967

I.

At 6:25 Monday night
eight uniformed policemen

escorted approximately 200
members of the Milwaukee

Youth Council of the NAACP
as they approached the north end

of the 16th Street Viaduct. Two
dozen Youth Council Commandos

flanked the marchers. The commandos
are Negro youths who act as security

guards for the youth council. Waiting
there was a contingent of parishioners

from St. Veronica Church on the far
south side, where Father James E. Groppi
once served as assistant pastor.

These 50 to 60 people held signs reading
"Welcome to the South Side" and joined in.

With the new numbers, the line started to bunch,
three, four, even five across.

COMMANDOs ran back and forth
the length of the line, urging
Keep it tight.
Don't bunch.
Two by two.

II.

At 9:25 p.m.
125 policemen
in riot helmets
5000 counter-demonstrators
235 marchers.

Lawrence: What Counts

That first night across the Viaduct
It was okay up front, but at the end,

everyone knows those are the people
the police, or the crowds, try to beat up on.

Well, maybe the St. Veronica's
folks didn't know that at first.

They learned.
We all learned as we went.

Pam: Crossing the 16th Street Viaduct

August 28, 1967

We left the 15th Street Freedom House singing
a full mile of freedom songs, right up to
the 16th Street Viaduct where more
people waited to join us.

But on the other side of the valley,
a hostile crowd ten times our numbers,
and the police.

This is Sgt. Miller of the Milwaukee Police Department.
Get back on the sidewalk. You do not have a parade permit.
By order of Harold Brier, Chief of Police.
Stay on the sidewalk or you will be arrested.

I marched next to Tommy Lee. He looked at me,
Pam, you stay on my right.
With a sweep of his arm,
he was between me and the crowd.

On the corner, a huge neon sign read
"Crazy Jim's Motors." Beneath the sign,
A mob of young White guys, jeering,
sitting on the hoods of the cars, holding signs,
awkward lettering on cardboard, "I want a slave."

The sleeves of his White undershirt were rolled
nearly to his shoulder, his chin jutted out, he sneered.
I could see he was missing a front tooth.

He clapped his hands, but whatever his chant
it was swallowed up by the noise of the crowd.
Tommy Lee grabbed my arm, yelled
Duck.

I turned to see why he yelled.
That's when I got hit. I grabbed my head.

See, the scar is still here. Even today.

Sometimes even today I can see the gap
where his tooth should have been. Can see
his face, though the rest of his crowd disappears.

Thank God.

Peggy: Crossing the 16th Street Viaduct

August 28, 1967

16th Street? No big deal.
In high school after football
or basketball games, we'd go to Pepi's.
Great pizza. We'd always find friends there.

Yet I couldn't be sure.
This was not high school, and I had new friends.
We marched past Pepi's.

I looked at the expanse of window.
I touched the glass. It was cool and smooth.
No one stood in this doorway.
No one glared at us through their windows.

I thought, it's okay. I know this place.
I'll be all right. We'll be all right.

I didn't look at the Crazy Jim's crowd. Too scary.
Up ahead was a stretch with fewer people.
When we get there, I thought, we'll be okay.

But something changed.
I felt like I had been in a tunnel
and was emerging into noise
like the noise of a crowd at a football game,
the noise of the home team's fans, and you're the visitor.

No. Listen. That's not it, not even close.
It's something deeper—
a wave of hate,
the sound of hate, blurring individual words.

We turned onto Lincoln Avenue,
the crowds thickening again. I couldn't ignore it anymore—
the blunt force of hate finding a rhyme and a rhythm:
I don't want a …jig… next door. Keep them in the inner core.

At Kosciusko Park, we huddled around picnic tables,
keeping very close, to be able to hear.
Some man, called himself district park supervisor,
said we couldn't give speeches.
A picnic permit, he shouted,
a picnic permit does not permit speeches.
We prayed, for peace, for justice, Father Groppi leading us.
Then back up Lincoln Avenue,
sometimes almost running.
police, night sticks angled up across their chests,
sometimes pushed back on people,
people trying to get at us.

The crowd noise was like a dome
enclosing us, the whole dome moving
rapidly down the street. My face was wet.
With sweat. I was not crying.

How had I walked these streets for years

and never seen the ugly?

Curley at Kosciusko Park

August 28, 1967

Some man, called himself district park supervisor,
said we couldn't give speeches. *A picnic permit,*
he shouted at Grop, *a picnic permit does not permit speeches.*

Father Groppi looked down from the table he was standing on,
said, *Are you going to clear our area and let us picnic?*
When you enforce the law on them, sweeping his arm around
toward the counter demonstrators, *you can enforce it on us.*

That hostile crowd was pushing on the police, closing in on us.
It was impossible to stay there, impossible to leave.
The police asked about bringing in a bus, but
what bus company would be crazy enough to take the job?

On the way to the park, I thought I'd never want
to see Crazy Jim's Motors again. On the way back,
I wondered if we would ever get there.

Jeannie's Birthday Gift

It was Jeannie's birthday. We
had a big family dinner before
going to St. Boniface to march.

She put on her new tee shirt, just
a plain White shirt, but what she wanted.
Mom said no, better not, but she begged

and begged 'til Mom gave in. She
never could wash out the egg that
splattered all over Jeannie's back.

Mary

August 29, 1967

Next night we were almost a thousand strong.
Wow. But for every one who joined us
looked like three or four more against us. Across
the Viaduct again, 16th Street, Kosciusko Park.
Marching, singing, praying, ducking, running.

Soon as we got back to the Freedom House,
police announced *disperse or you will be arrested.*
What? We just got here.
How to make sense with all the noise.
Too much talking inside the house.
Too much shouting outside.
Too many sirens in the distance, closing in.

Then through it all a policeman yelled,
Sniper. There's a sniper.
All of a sudden, his rifle was at his shoulder.
He started shooting, shot out the streetlight.
Glass shattered. More. Boom, boom, boom.
Clouds of tear gas. The whole area.
Then right in the Freedom House.

Flames shot up inside the house.
We ran out.
I couldn't see any more.
I knew not to rub my eyes.

I hollered for Daddy.
I didn't know where Nibby was.

Or Junior.
I couldn't breathe.
I started retching
like I was going to throw up.

Daddy grabbed my hand and pulled me.
I started running with him.
When we looked back,
the house was engulfed in flames.
All those sirens. Police.
Not a fire truck to be found.

Toward a Poetry of Fact

The Milwaukee Sentinel
Wednesday, August 30, 1967

Fire chiefs reported difficulty getting to the scene of the
fire last night at the Milwaukee NAACP Youth Council
headquarters at 1316 North 15th Street because key
thoroughfares were closed.

Cause of the fire is disputed. Police fired tear gas canisters
to disperse the crowd which they said was unruly.

Youth Council spokesman Nathaniel Harwell said one
of the canisters exploded when it hit the wood floor and
ignited. The flames spread through the old wood of the
structure rapidly. Before the night was over, all that was
left of the 15th Street Freedom House was a charred and
crumbling frame.

Closed. Cause. Canisters. Crowd.

Crumbling. Frame. Fire. Flames. Freedom.

Mary's Mother

Milwaukee August 29, 1967

When my babies got home,
got home safe that night, I cried.
Thank you, Jesus.

Lord, those people.
You should have seen them on TV, yelling
go back to Africa.
Throwing rocks and bottles, cursing.
What's the matter with them?

Next morning soon as the girls came down stairs
I got them to work.
Mary Ann, you listen to me, Mary Ann.
You get some breakfast yourself.
Then fry up some eggs for Nibby and Junior.

Nibby, you just smiling, so sweet,
and I want you to keep smiling, just like that.
It's a new day, even if they don't know it.

Yes, that's good, Honey. Yes, the frying pan's right there.
I talked with your daddy last night. I said, *Dave,*
I'm not having these children out there again tonight
by themselves. He knew exactly what I was talking about.

Now wash your hands, Mary Ann.
Get that raw egg cleaned up. That's right.

I need to get on the phone, call Auntie May,
Auntie Esther, Mr. and Mrs. Butler, the Wrays.
We got to get some adults out there with you.
We're not having you children out there
again tonight by yourselves. Tear gas.
People screaming *we want slaves*.
Those people are crazy. Lord almighty!

That's good, Mary Ann.
You flip those eggs nice and gentle.
Junior, hand me the phone.

Vel's Villanelle

Henry issued a proclamation forbidding marches.
Henry Maier, the mayor.
We couldn't march. He saw to that.

Just as Groppi says: when there's a riot on
the north side, the mayor calls for the National Guard.
He issues a proclamation imposing a curfew on us.

When there's a riot on the south side,
when White people are screaming to kill Black people,
then it's we who can't march. Henry saw to that.

Groppi was angry but said okay, the Youth Council will not
march. We'll just meet at the Freedom House to plan.
Henry issued a proclamation forbidding marches.

Your presence is important, Vel, he told me.
It'll add dignity. That's what he said.
We couldn't march. Henry had seen to that.

Police announced to us at the Freedom House
This is an illegal gathering. You are violating the law.
Apparently Henry issued a proclamation forbidding marchers

everything. *Disperse or you will be arrested.*
Those who tried to leave were also immediately arrested.
We couldn't even gather. Henry had seen to that.

COMMANDOs formed a wedge to protect
Grop and me. They were charged, resisting arrest
and violating the proclamation Henry issued.
We couldn't protest. Henry had seen to that.

Curley Learns

We all went before Seraphim.
Judge Seraphim.

Belongs to the Eagle's Club
with its Whites only clause.

You in here again? he said to me.
I'm sick of seeing you. When will you learn?

Yeah. I wanted to tell him
"sick of you" is a two way street.

Pam and Shirley's New Verse

They say that Mayor Maier
Has gone and lost his mind
He went and bought some Coppertone
And tried to join our picket line.

Pam On the Third Try

My grandmother didn't want me participating.
She thought I was in my room.
She was watching the TV that night,

she sees me being thrown in a paddy wagon.
I thought I can't get arrested, and tried to jump back out.
Three times.

Three times they threw me back in,
the TV camera catching all of this.
If she had any doubt was it me on the first time,

she saw for sure on the second and third tries.
She came down, my grandmother did,
soon as I called her, came down to get me.

She was mad, but she came to get me.
All the way out to juvenile detention.
And that was one thing she never yelled about.

And a man has not begun to live until he can rise above the narrow confines of his own individual concerns to the broader concerns of all humanity.

—The Rev. Dr. Martin Luther King Jr.
April 9, 1967

Her name was Nancy.

She moved in just a couple of weeks ago.
I had carried her couch up four flights of stairs.
I said hello. She smiled, was friendly,
but didn't know me from a doorknob.

How could she have forgotten?
It had been 90 some degrees.
Only a couple of people were helping.
I knew one of them. He said,
Chuck, we need you.

Our hands grew sweaty, trying to hold on
to that monster couch up all those stairs.
It's true that I didn't see her again until
the night of the march down our street.

What a noise in the street! Loud.
I mean really loud. I looked out,
saw a surge of people, the marchers, calling out,
Y'all, come on. Join the march to freedom.

I saw Nancy walk out the front door,
join them, headed toward the 16th Street viaduct.
To this day I tell myself I picked up my keys
ran down to join because I believed in this cause.

Another friend introduced us.
I said we already met. Don't you remember

the couch? The four flights of stairs?

Five Gestures for Freedom

Friday, September 1, 1967
for Mark Lococo

Arms locked to step into street.

Arms over head, protection against billy clubs.

Hands to face cupped around mouth
doubled over, retching. Tear gas.

Elbows up, angled out, pulled into arrest.

Arms behind back, wrists caught in handcuffs.

Mark Rosenman remembers

after a few years at the NAACP, a promotion
NAACP Youth and College Division Director.

Meetings all day, phone calls
stay late at night for time, space, equipment
copy, staple, send out fliers. Weekends
Hartford. Oklahoma City. Orangeburg. Springfield.

Finally a chance for vacation. Leave
at the end of the busy summer, August
Return, maybe, maybe mid-September.

New York, a plane
California, a college friend
Mexico, a quiet hotel.

We do not speak the language
We manage with a phrase book
with a smile, nod or shake of the head.

Day one: a stroll around the square
a low key dinner, uninterrupted sleep
no phone, no mail, no politics, no strategizing.

Day two: a nearby bakery. Fresh rolls
A newspaper on the table. Why did I look?
On the front page, a photo

police, demonstrators, a house on fire
One word that needs no translation
Milwaukee.

Oh, shit.

Ballade of Dick Gregory

Comedian Dick Gregory announced
he will arrive tonight to join the marchers.
The Milwaukee Sentinel, Saturday, September 2, 1967

The image of a house on fire
flashes across the nightly news
from coast to coast. Mayor Maier
plays well at home but he loses
national support when he excuses
overt racist actions. *Join the fight,*
exhorts the NAACP. Thousands do.
Dick Gregory arrives to march tonight.

He comes with an intense desire
for fair housing, freedom to choose.
He quickly learns that Harold Brier,
like Jim Clark or Bull Connor, pursues
his ends with clubs and gas. He issues
orders, employs might against right.
Unworried, undaunted, always enthused,
Dick Gregory says he'll march tonight.

His spirit recharges those who had tired.
He brings new ideas, new tools,
experience the Youth Council admires.
He praises what we've begun. He argues
for this much needed law. Reviews
how boycotts helped the Birmingham fight.
Says *boycott Schlitz,* top Milwaukee brew.
Dick Gregory joins our cause tonight.

Let's go, he says. Who can refuse?
Down Twelfth to North, the line stays tight.
Nearby police clench clubs, tear gas they'll use.
Dick Gregory rallies hope on this march tonight.

Ninety Acres of Courage

I always knew they were with me. With us.
My granddaddy Aaron Hazelwood in Belzoni, Mississippi
called Daddy, said *look like Mary Ann on TV.*
On the national news.

He and Granny knew I was arrested before my parents did.
They were in the movement themselves.
Gave freedom riders a place to stay
when no one else would.
Called all movement folks *freedom riders.*

Fact is we were down there once when we were little.
One night there was this big fire down the road.
Granddaddy say *you girls just keep jumping rope.*

We say but Granddaddy, what's this burning?
It's nothing, Baby. Don't worry, Mary Ann.
You and Nibby keep jumping rope.

Later, years later, they told us.
The Ku Klux Klan right there,
there at my grandfather's place.

He couldn't read or write,
but he owned ninety acres
free and clear. Raised cotton.
Wasn't afraid of nobody.

It happened to him once before, too.
The Ku Klux Klan trying to scare him.
He didn't scare.

When we joined the movement, it was like
he came back to life.

Change the Game

In August Mayor Maier blocked our march
by issuing a proclamation. Chief Brier
was quick to jail us. Then our numbers surged.
The aldermen complained, *you wreck our rep-
utation as a place that's fair.* Their fair.

In fall their strategy turned cold. They dup-
licated a weak Wisconsin statute
exempting owner-occupied and small
buildings, exactly what Milwaukee had.
We marched for something stronger, fair for all.

Year's end. Cameras turn toward Green Bay,
the Packers, minus twenty cold, last play—
a sneak, they win—fans ecstatic!

We huddle, keep our line tight, our eyes on our goal.

School Lessons

Young Lady, you're not
appropriately dressed.
Look at me when I'm talking to you.
You will not be permitted in this classroom.
Go right to the office.

Young Lady, you're not
appropriately dressed.
No incendiary slogans in school.
We have to call your mother,
send you home to change

That's all right, Mary.
They just told us again
how they are. Not
that we didn't know already.
Freedom Now…incendiary….

Oh, Lord, the very idea!

Milwaukee Talks II

Did you hear? Father Groppi got a new calendar.
January, February, March, March, March.

Weapons

Father Groppi took me to the Father – Daughter dinner
at St. Joan Antida High School. His idea of a high school for me.
But I didn't know he had taught there.

Folks there could be strange. Didn't know how they'd react to him.
I put a steak knife in my purse. Didn't let my grandmother see.
Didn't want her to know. Didn't want him to know.

I wanted to be ready. Just in case.

But the nuns all knew him from his having taught there.
He told me, *Pam, you have crazy ideas sometimes.*
No more knives in the purse. Promise me.

Yeah, but he got a gun from a priest friend of his,
worried about answering the door at night.
Couldn't not answer it, he said, because it might be one of us.
But it might also be some crazy bigot.

He'd answer the door with the pistol in his back pocket.
Curley said, one of these mornings I'm going to pick up
the paper, and see the headline:
Father Groppi Shoots Himself in the Buttocks.

We Felt Like Losers

March 19, 1968, the 200th night

Where? Who? What? When?
For 200 nights the Milwaukee NAACP Youth Council
on the bridge, in the jails, at the city limits, in Seraphim's court
What will it take? How in our life?

After 200 nights the Milwaukee Youth Council
Momentum gone, money gone
What will it take? How in our life?
How closed their minds? How hard their hearts?

Momentum gone, money gone
wondering what future, what next month.
What closed the minds? What hardened the hearts?
What to say when it's not over, but it ends?

Wondering what future, what tomorrow,
how to bridge such injustice, counter such limits
what to say to move mayor, to upend denial.
What? Who? Where? When?

We Interrupt This Program

April 4, 1968

It was evening, but I was just getting up.
I worked third shift, welding, in Cedarburg.
A bus picked us up about 10:15,
sometimes the bus was late, picked us up
at an office on Third Street,
brought us back to Milwaukee
when our shift ended at 7:00.

Cella, my wife Celeste, had dinner about ready.
Lorenzo had already gone down for the night.
I turned on the TV. It was all over the news:
Martin Luther King's been shot in Memphis.
Seriously wounded. Taken to the hospital. No word yet....

We interrupt this program.

"Cella," I said.
I could see her in the kitchen.
She didn't move. She stood at the stove,
her fork in her hand, her hand in midair,
the pan sizzling, the smell of fried chicken almost too much.
I opened my mouth like I had something to say,
but what was there to say?
What words would say
what Celeste and I already said to each other
without a word?

Finally I got up, put on my jacket, started for the door.
"I can't eat." It was all I could say.
"Lawrence." It was all Cella could say.
She said it deep so all at once it said
of course, and *take care,*
how could they, and *what next.*
She said it so I loved her more than ever.
She knew where I was going.
St. Boniface.

On the streets, taking the pulse,
the talk: Baltimore, Chicago,
Washington tore up already,
as if to set us off, too.
Even at the church: *should we….*

No. Shirley, Mary, and I
cut off that question right at the stem.

Instead we plan: tomorrow
Mass at St. Boniface.
Then Milwaukee will march
in his honor. His way.
The next day a bus to Atlanta.

Out again into the streets,
to the bars, spreading the word.
Tomorrow. St. Boniface.

I forgot about the bus to work.
We walked down 12th to Locust, then to Third.
Stopped in all the bars until a bartender told us,

You guys can go home.
The mayor issued an order.
All bars are to close immediately.

Who knew the time? The bus pulled up.
Someone said, *I'll call Celeste for you.*
The ride was unusually quiet.
The men nodded at me.
St. Boniface. Tomorrow.

Word was getting word around.
I watched the dark streets slip out of sight.
Whatever mess was going on in Baltimore,
Washington or Chicago was not
going on here in Milwaukee.
There was tomorrow.

Love on the March

M'dear looked at them, said, *no, no way.*
We'd be talking about some boys we thought so cute.

My dad told me, *Shirley, you keep your butt covered.*
We'd be talking. Some were crazy, but some were cute.
All I knew about sex was keep your butt covered
and you won't get pregnant. And I was eighteen years old.

We'd be flirting with some boy we thought really cute.
M'dear kept an eye on us, said, *no, no way.*

Aftermath

St. Boniface. We packed that church.
It rocked.
St. Boniface school. We learned.
The playground, teargassed.

The rectory, fell to the wrecking ball.
The church. All torn down.

A reporter asked Ken Burgess,
financial director for the Archbishop,
Will you sell St. Boniface?

Burgess answered,
If the price is right.
The price was right.

I wonder what that price was.
What is history worth anyway?

The Impregnable Poetry
of the Supreme Court

Groppi v. Wisconsin, 400 U.S. 505 (1971)

STEWART, J., delivered the opinion of the Court, in which DOUGLAS, HARLAN, BRENNAN, WHITE, and MARSHALL, JJ., joined. BLACKMUN, J., filed a concurring opinion, in which BURGER, C.J., joined.

Here, we are concerned with the methods available to assure an impartial jury in a situation where, because of prejudicial publicity or for some other reason, the community from which the jury is to be drawn may already be permeated with hostility toward the defendant. The problem is an ancient one. Mr. Justice Holmes stated no more than a commonplace when, two generations ago, he noted that

"[a]ny judge who has sat with juries knows that, in spite of forms, they are extremely likely to be impregnated by the environing atmosphere." *Frank v. Mangum,* 237 U. S. 309, 237 U. S. 349 (dissenting opinion).

MR. JUSTICE BLACKMUN, whom THE CHIEF JUSTICE joins, concurring.

Finally, I doubt very much whether this rather unimportant case, but an admittedly sensitive one because of the identity of the defendant and the means he has selected to make his protests known, at all approaches the circumstances and the offensive character of what this Court condemned in *Sheppard v. Maxwell,* 384 U. S. 333 (1966), in *Rideau v. Louisiana,* 373 U. S. 723 (1963), and in *Irvin v. Dowd,* 366 U. S. 717 (1961), cited in the Court's opinion. Nevertheless, unfairness anywhere, in small cases as well as in large, is abhorred, is to be ferreted out, and is to be eliminated.

Calling the Roll

Sylvester, Clyde, Tommy Lee
What can these names mean to you?
David, Lawrence, Vada, and Jimmy

They marched to open up Milwaukee
when Whites only was the general rule.
Sullivan, Carol, Ed, and Lee

Jailed, they went with dignity.
Cursed, they never lost their cool.
DeWayne, Mrs. Campbell, Mr. McGhee

Few their moments of applause or publicity.
Overlooked, they still did what they had to.
Robert, Cheryl, John, and Naomi

Here's to their validation finally.
They're the model of what we all can do.
Rev. Kirkendol, Mrs. Yarborough, Father Groppi

Brothers and sisters, in your names a panoply
of meaning. You crossed a bridge and made news.
You built a bridge and made history,
Sylvester, Clyde, and Tommy Lee.

On the Bridge

for Stephen Hennessey Cooney, 1977–2004

In my favorite photo ten-year old Stephen, sun
touching his patient face, the sleeve of his blue shirt, holds
close to him a boy half his age, half his size, half

his calm. His left arm cradles the shoulder, his right
hand encircled by the fingers of the boy who squints,
his skin like a peach absorbing the heat of the sun

as he seems intent on some mischief
Stephen overlooks. In the background
Stephen's skateboard propped against a fence,

beyond that the freeway, traffic streaming beneath
them. They await the celebration opening
Milwaukee's James E. Groppi Unity Bridge.

Since calm grows more and more difficult to find
I relish this moment there, there, where time
had space, where boys had hope and almost stood still.

Toward an Epilogue

I am the old person.
A young audience sits before me,
wondering about these old times,
back in the day....

These places to them flat lines:
St. Boniface, the 15th Street Freedom House,
the 16th Street Viaduct. Kosciusko Park.

The oval of this auditorium.
Oblong bodies curved into the right-angled seats.
Anticipation arcing over this hour
to the next and on to the next.

Faces mostly round.
Mouths. Theirs. And mine ...
I take a deep breath, speak
deliberately as if pumping air into a flat tire.

I marched for open housing in Milwaukee.
Shirley, Mary, Barb, Nibby, Junior,
Curley, Lawrence, Peabody, Ed,
we marched across the 16th Street viaduct.
Two hundred of us.
At the south end of the viaduct
we met a hostile wall,
5000 counter-demonstrators.

The tangents of the present recede,
their square roots being factored

out of abstract math and into the geometry
of the picket line, the architecture
of courthouse and jail cell,
the calculus of rallies, marches,
legislation drafted, resisted, compromised,
filibustered, amended, debated.

The rise of a reverberating chorus.
Determination. Drive. Energy.
The elliptical pitch of lives rolling on ideals.
One hand plus one hand
one arm around another's shoulders.

We marched on when the city fathers
were all "business as usual"
We marched on when some supporters
 said *you need to pick another issue.*

We did what we knew we had to do.
Through all the heat.
Through all the rain.
Through all that nasty cold.
When the crowds went home.
We marched on
'til victory was won.

Hey, y'all. We DID it! We did IT!
WE did it!

Crank up the music there, Peabody.
Another generation sits here waiting.

Epilogue

Between the living of this story of the Milwaukee open hous-
ing campaign and the telling of it lie forty years. In August
1967 when Father James Groppi led the Milwaukee Youth
Council of the NAACP across Milwaukee's 16th Street via-
duct to the virtually all-White South Side, I was one of the
older members of that Youth Council, having just earned my
bachelor's degree at Alverno College. When Martin Luther
King was martyred on April 4, 1968 and when first Congress
(April 12th) and then the Milwaukee Common Council
(April 30th) finally passed open housing legislation, I was in
my first year as a teacher at North Division High School.

Today I am a professor of English at the University of
Wisconsin-Waukesha. In between was the peace movement,
graduate school, marriage, establishing a family, being wid-
owed, and then as the single parent of three children, strug-
gling with the anger and grief precipitated by great loss.

Anger propels you forward; grief slows you down, maybe
puts you into reverse. In this sort of halting way, I prepared
classes, graded student essays, scurried with children to
their bus stop, went to their swimming meets, and tried to
instill in them a sense of social justice. They grew up with
freedom songs for lullabies and, when their dad died, they
learned to fish with the help of friends who had marched
across the viaduct with us.

Having lived this history means continuing to live it. It
is always there, part and parcel of who we are. Over the
course of forty years, Barb, Pam, Mary, Shirley, I and many
others who had crossed that viaduct together never lost our

sense of those powerful friendships. We renewed our stories when we gathered together, too often for funerals. After St. Boniface Church was torn down, we relied on the intangible but profound sense of church we had with each other.

The name of my husband, Father James Groppi, continues to hold power in Milwaukee, to serve as a reference point. In this city, to say you marched with Father Groppi, or your parents or grandparents did, is to establish your civil rights credentials.

Given this setting and background, when civil rights literature and histories began to appear in print and on my desk, I was astonished to read that they generally concluded with the 1965 March for Voting Rights from Selma to Montgomery, Alabama, the time when my own civil rights activity was just beginning. I was also puzzled that so few mention any civil rights movement in the North.

Framing the civil rights story in this way leaves many confirmed civil rights activists out of the picture. To tell the civil rights story narrowly helps fuel the commonly held notion that it is a closed book with nothing to say to us today. To insist that the larger dimensions of the story be recognized helps to make that story empowering. Young people today can look at the ordinary teenagers who appear in these poems, who somehow found the courage to stand up for justice, and say, "I can do that too."

I wasted too much time being angry. I had a wonderful story to tell, to celebrate, and I wanted to use all the resources of language and literary form to tell it well. Thanks to Mark Lococo, then associate professor and theater director at the University of Wisconsin-Waukesha, the story first took form as a play, a documentary drama called *March On Milwaukee: A Memoir of the Open Housing Protests.*

Thanks to others, especially Mario Hall, Andre Ellis and Maripat Wilkinson, the play had additional productions in the city of Milwaukee where some wanted to forget how Milwaukee became the "Selma of the North," with jeering crowds resisting civil rights. Others were sorry for their ignorance or lack of courage, and many others celebrated that this story with their names and the names of their loved ones finally was being told so that a new generation would know we had tried to create for them, with two hundred plus nights of marching, a better world.

But theatrical productions are expensive. They require actors, a stage, scenery and props, a director, rehearsal time, and lighting and sound technicians. And I am primarily a poet.

For some parts of the story of the Milwaukee marches, poetic form instantly and clearly was the right vehicle for the story. When some parts seemed less amenable to poetry, I had to ask myself, what is poetry? What does poetry have to do with the who, what, when, where, and how of journalistic facts? One answer is in "Toward a Poetry of Fact." The two concluding lines pull alliterative terms from the more reportorial body of the poem and set them forth as the poetic heart distilled from fact.

Handbooks of poetic form helped when the writing stalled or stubbornly refused to budge from the prosaic. The poems in this collection include many poetic forms, among them the sonnet, villanelle, pantoum, ballade, and cinquain.

Almost none of them follows exactly the traditional formal rules. "Change the Game," for example, is a sonnet, but it abandons rhyme and divides into units of five, five, three and one lines. This formal flexibility is metaphorical. What the open housing marches did for set territorial boundaries in Milwaukee these poems do with traditional poetic forms.

The old boundaries are questioned, rearranged, expanded, and maybe abandoned.

These poems also identify a certain Lannon stone intractability as prose, or prosaic. Conversely a Supreme Court decision, apparently prose, reaffirms principles of justice and is thus identified with poetry. I don't know about making this an absolute, but as both a poet and a civil rights activist, this identification is central to my experience. I believe what Leslie Marmon Silko affirms in *Ceremony*: "Stories are the only thing we have to keep from sickness and death." Moreover, I believe they are all we need.

— Margaret Rozga

Acknowledgments

Grateful acknowledgment to **Main Street Rag** in which "Shirley's Mother" was previously published.

A special thank you to all those who helped bring this book to reality especially Marianne Roccaforte, who inspires; friend and mentor, poet Lois Roma-Deeley who believed this story needed to be told even when she read its earliest versions; Carolyn Muchhala, Helen Padway, Mara Ptacek, Phyllis Wax, Ellen Bravo, Sandy Brusin, Kris Terwelp, and Leslie Whitaker who critiqued rough drafts; editor Sydney James, who tended lovingly to every word; publishers Le Roy Chappell and Lesly Chappell for their commitment to social justice and their belief in the transformative power of literature.

My deepest gratitude to all those who lived with courage, grace, and dignity the story this book tells, especially those who continue to march on with me: Pamela Sargent, Mary Childs Arms, Adolph Arms, James Arms, Shirley Butler-Derge, Fred Reed, Barbara David Salas, Ronald Britton, Norma Britton, the Honorable Vel R. Phillips, and, most of all, the Rev. James E. Groppi.

About Benu Press

Benu Press is a small, independent press committed to publishing poetry, fiction, and creative non-fiction. We believe in the transformative power of literature. To that end, we seek to publish inspiring and thought-provoking books about the practical dimensions of social justice and equity.

Also published by Benu Press
All Screwed Up, Steve Fellner

For more information about Benu Press
http:// www.benupress.com

℮

For more information about the events in this book
http://www.marchonmilwaukee.org/
http://wbhsm.homestead.com/marchonmilwaukee.html